WIZARDS OF SUCCESS

SENORITA JOYCE

To my Mom, Joyce

who has always been supportive,

not only of this book but my whole life,

Love you Mom, To the moon and back.

Contents

Foreword

Regardless of how you define success -- be it financial, spiritual, physical, mental, emotional, philanthropic, communal or familial -- the most important thing you must know about success in order to have success are the following:

1. Success is important;
2. Success is your obligation.
3. Success is your duty.

Regardless of culture, race, religion, economic background or social group, most would agree that success is important and vital to the well-being of the individual, the family unit, the group and certainly to the survival of those things into the future. Those that minimize the importance of success are either confused or have given up on their own chances of success.

Success provides confidence, security, a sense of well-being, the ability to contribute at a greater level, hope and leadership. Without success, you, the group, your company, your goals, dreams and even entire civilizations cease to survive. Without continued success, the company, dream, even entire races will cease to exist, as was the case with the Vikings, Romans, Greeks, American Indians and then an endless list of companies and products. Success is important in that it is required in order to continue on!

Preface

Success should never be reduced to something that does not matter or isn't important. It is *vital* and should be held as such! If you are unable to succeed in taking care of your children, they will be taken over by the state. For an individual or group to continue on, he or she must actively accomplish his or her goals and targets (succeed) or he or she will cease to exist. For a business or industry to continue on, it must be successful in creating new products, getting those products to the market, keeping clients, employees and investors happy and repeating that cycle, over and over.

Cute sayings that somehow dismiss the importance of success abound, like, "Success is a journey, not a destination." Please! When your future viability is threatened, these cute little sayings will prove to be poor substitution for success. The last couple of years of economic turmoil should have made it obvious that we all underestimated how much success is needed and how valuable it actually is to our survival and well-being.

Regardless of what goals you are trying to attain, success is important. Quit succeeding, and you quit winning; quit winning long enough, and you will quit! Do your kids benefit when they see mom and daddy losing? Does anyone benefit when you can't get your art sold, or you can't get that great book published, or you have some great idea that will improve the world, but can't succeed in bringing it to the world?

Success isn't just important; it is *vital*, and should never be reduced to anything less than vital. Success is valuable, important and necessary for survival.

Acknowledgements

I blame all of you, collating this book has been such an agony. A casual reader may perhaps, exempt themselves from excessive guilt. But for those of you who have supported me throughout and have been my strenght (Oscar, Oliver, Oreo, Sunny, Rocky and Dad) I owe this to you guys.

Prologue

Why success is important in life? It won't be a hard question to answer because In today's society in which we live, without a doubt, one of the most important elements of progress and living is success.

Each of us has a unique idea of what success is. Your success is getting what you want for your life, what you have set out to do, be it winning a competition, getting a job, having a relationship, starting a business, earning money for some goal, or quitting smoking.

In personal life, at work, in the decisions you make, in the way you manage your own economy: success is present in everything, and it becomes almost one of the only engines that move us.

Other values such as solidarity, ideology or courage, weigh less and less. Our actions are often marked in large part by our pursuit of success.

About The Author

SENORITA JOYCE - A Professional who thrives on helping others by going above and beyond with every task She's given. An enthusiast about growing and gaining new skills in her professional journey.She love's to hear about other people's passion and interests and also how she could possibly be of help. And to top it all, She value's learning from everyone She meet's throughout her journey. She's a genuine believer in getting the work done by smiling, laughing and even twirling at times.

Being a Motivational Speaker She firmly believe's in the law of attraction and loves to read self help books and One of her all time favorite is "As a Man Thinketh" by James Allen.

Outside of Work She's a huge Coffee nerd & a Published Author with 6 books so far selling on Flipkart & Amazon, namely 'One Step at a Time, 'A-Z of Positivity', 'Wanderlust' & 'Journals by My AI Friend', 'Coach Yourself to Happiness', 'Indian Dance - Expression without Speech'. Being on the creative side She also love painting, 20 of which have been exhibited so far and the proceeds to which goes towards different social causes she works for.

Currently the VP | Corporate Trainer with one of the Leading Ed-Space Start-up, A budding Entrepreneur, Has been invited as Keynote Speaker on various occasions for IIT-Mumbai, Also the Global Goodwill Ambassador for India, and the Columnist for one of India's leading Webzine "Namaste India" and management Magazine "Startocure". She believes that it is ones moral obligation to benefit the society that's where her Social work comes into picture, Volunteering with various NGOs working towards Women empowerment, child rights, RTE and Animal Welfare, A Doctorate Holder & An IIM-Rohtak, Alumni.

CHAPTER ONE

BELIEVE IT TO SEE IT

We can be our biggest cheerleaders — or our biggest critics. And the difference between the two options matters. Believing in yourself is crucial to succeeding.

Self-efficacy, or your ability to believe in yourself, can improve your success in goal setting. Studies have looked at how higher self-efficacy indicates success in areas like academic performance or quitting smoking. If you can believe, you really can achieve.

It helps to adopt a growth mindset and cultivate the ability to accept and learn from your mistakes. Developing these characteristics can take patience and time.

Self-belief is the formula to personal and professional success.

Do you berate yourself when you make a mistake? Do you, for some reason or other, think negative self-talk will make you a better person?

Making mistakes is one thing. But at some point, you have to forgive yourself and move on. Otherwise, that energy will only hold you back. It'll prevent you from taking risks and stepping up to achieve your goals.

At the end of the day, you have to believe in yourself. Doing so will bring you one step closer to manifesting a better life.

Here's why you should believe in yourself and your instincts:

1. If you don't, who else will?

Maybe you have a system of people who love and support you, and that's great. But at the end of the day, only you can act on the opportunities in your life. At some point in your life, you'll have to take a leap of faith. And you'll have to trust in your ability to survive it.

2. You'll fail more gracefully

Look, it happens to all of us. Even the most successful people know what failure feels like. But they know that, as long as they learn something, they'll continue to grow. You can be like that, too — you just have to trust yourself.

3. Being follows doing (sometimes you have to act positive to get positive)

If you don't believe you're worthy, neither will other people. You have to suspend your disbelief and take the leap to act like you believe in yourself, first. You'll see yourself through new eyes and so will other people.

Negativity begets negativity. That's why you should flip the script. When you show more positivity, you'll attract more positive people in your life.

4. You'll inspire yourself to keep going

You'll encounter all sorts of obstacles in life. You'll feel tired, wary, and want to quit. But if you believe in yourself, you'll look back on all your previous successes and remember that better is possible.

5. You'll start reaching your goals

How can you reach your goals if you don't even think you can? Your successes shouldn't be a surprise, they should be a validation of your belief in yourself. Believing in yourself helps you focus and increases productivity. Positive thinking is infectious, and it'll spread to others, inspiring them to believe in themselves.

Positive self-talk is easier said than done. You must control your thoughts, feelings, and actions. Rewiring your brain to think positive thoughts in the place of criticism is tricky.

Three common roadblocks people face regarding self-belief are:

1. Comparison

Perception is everything. Seeing someone else thriving doesn't mean you aren't.

Remember, what you see on social media is what people let you see, and they don't tend to advertise their struggles. It's like that old saying: Don't compare your insides to someone else's outside.

Plus, there's room for both you and your peers to thrive. Feel proud of friends and colleagues that are doing well, without succumbing to envy.

2. The past

There's some truth to the phrase, "The past can haunt you." It's hard to shake off a rough childhood or an unhealthy relationship. Self-reflection is good, but not at the expense of your mental health. Talking to a mental health professional is a great way to work through your past struggles and stop them from affecting your present.

3. Current relationships

Do you have that one friend that's always putting you down? Maybe it's a parent or a colleague that you dread seeing because they make you feel small. Human beings are social creatures by nature, but a lack of approval can be detrimental to your self-confidence.

How to overcome roadblocks

Remember, roadblocks aren't permanent obstacles — there's always a way past them. Try these strategies:

Think positively: Your thoughts make up a large part of who you are and what you do. Believing in yourself and your abilities to tackle any hurdle is an essential step to beating whatever you're up against.

Visualize where you want to be: This will keep you motivated, even when things look bleak and self-doubt sets in. While you can't change the past, you can make a better future. Whatever you want to do is possible.

Take action: Thinking and "talking the talk" are important but eventually, you must "walk the walk." You'll feel better about yourself and your skills as you make progress and see the rewards that arise from the work you're putting in to make a change.

7 strategies that will help you believe in yourself

Don't let the obstacles discourage you. Below are seven ways to make a change and feel better about yourself:

1. Create healthy routines

Living well is critical to loving yourself. Feeding your body with healthy food and drink, exercising, sleeping, and taking breaks amidst your work schedule are all important. Your anxiety will decrease, and you can tackle each day with more strength. Self-love is all about maintaining a balance and doing all you can to set yourself up for success.

2. Surround yourself with good people

Public speaker and self-help guru Tony Robbins says, "Proximity is power." There's truth in that. The people you spend time with have an impact on your mindset and your motivation. Seek out people who inspire you to be your best self and the ones who help you get there.

Encouraging individuals will keep you going when things get hard, and they'll challenge you, too.

Be on the lookout for people with these toxic personality traits. If you find yourself drained, negative, and full of self-doubt around certain people, spend less time with them. Cut them out of your life. If that's not possible, do your best to limit time spent together.

3. Feed your mind

There's some truth to the law of attraction, too — the type of energy you give off comes back to you, positive and negative. While it might not really be a natural law, it's true that your mindset affects how you interact with the world and how other people interact with you.

What you fill your mind with influences how you see yourself and the world around you.

Seek out inspiring and uplifting media, from books to movies to social media accounts. Frequent exposure to uplifting and supportive material will slowly condition your brain to think differently. Limit your time with overly pessimistic or cynical perspectives. While it's important to be realistic and embrace the ups and downs of life, cynicism erodes your belief in others, destroys your motivation, and takes away your hope for the future. It doesn't help how you feel about yourself, either.

4. Don't let your fear stop you

Self-doubt is normal. You can't let that hold you back. Speak up. Set goals. Learning something new or overcoming a hurdle releases dopamine in your brain, and you'll physically feel better with each step you take. Instead of feeling frustrated or small when errors occur, remember that you can learn from mistakes. That is, setbacks are also a potential source of growth.

5. Draw on your inner strength

Sometimes pushing through is all you can do. Just because you fail at a task doesn't mean you're a failure. Dig deep for grit, and keep going even in challenging moments.

6. Acknowledge your victories

Celebrate the little things and the big accomplishments. Celebrate your passions. Instead of being self-critical, opt to practice self-compassion.

7. Work on your strengths

When you're feeling down in the dumps, it's common to focus on your weaknesses. Instead, work to identify your strengths. It can help to ask others for feedback. Then, focus on honing those skills — it'll help you feel more capable.

The bottom line

Self-care is often put on the back burner in favor of other responsibilities, but believing in yourself is just one aspect of our well-being.

Everyone is unique, full of possibility, capable of self-improvement, and worthy of self-belief. Using technology, world-class coaching, and evidence-based behavioral science, we strive to help every individual unlock their greater potential and purpose.

CHAPTER TWO

OBSTACLES ARE A WONDERFUL GIFT

Obstacles suck. They are what you try to avoid or work around. Obstacles are where the flow of things gets bottled up; where things break down, or where you feel most out of alignment. Yet they play an important role in the progression of any story.

What are you trying to create in the world? Are you are a change agent, the leader of an organization, an entrepreneur? In nearly every organization or business, the language and experience of obstacles is playing out, no matter how carefully you plan, who you hire, or what you're selling.

Obstacles are Critical to the Hero's Journey

Your first response to obstacles is often to demonize them.

The language we use is often militaristic (e.g. attack that problem, conquer the challenge). It's easy to have negative emotion toward what's going wrong. So much so that it makes you want to avoid dealing with it. Often times, people know the bottleneck, constraint, or problem is there but no one wants to deal with it. Obstacles then turn into gremlins who've been fed after midnight.

Despite the furry devils, obstacles can be a tremendous gift on your path. You can't discover, reveal, or embrace the full nature of your character without them. In fact, obstacles are the places where character is forged and revealed; they offer the perfect opportunities for you and your business to grow and become better aligned and more smoothly flowing. When you can embrace your obstacles, you invite the process of growth and transformation.

Sometimes the sheer number of obstacles you face can seem overwhelming, to the point of obscuring the path forward. Which ones really matter? How do you choose which obstacles to face and which ones to ignore? These are difficult choices.

Here are three strategies to consider. The sooner you begin to see your obstacles as a gift that will help you move forward, the sooner you'll graduate the next level of your game.

1. Embrace the Discomfort

Transformation in any story comes from stepping out of your comfort zone. Imagine if Frodo never left the Shire. Or if King George of Britain never confronted his stutter. In hero's journey terms, the protagonist at first often ignores the call to adventure. Yet eventually you reach a point where you must leave the place of comfort and step out into the wilderness.

Rarely do we opt into a place of discomfort. We have to be nudged there by either yearning or frustration. Typically we wince away from something that hurts, but the first step in seeing obstacles as a gift is to lean into the discomfort. In storytelling terms, you want heat. Look for the heat. The best stories emerge out of the smoking cauldron of creative tension.

The key to look for is "emotional overhead." What are issues, subjects, or topics that are hard for you to discuss? What's considered taboo or off-limits within your organization? What are the biggest areas of frustration or bottleneck? Those are the smoke signals for you to pay attention to.

You can't be afraid to get close to this fire. Accept the fact that you will likely get burned. Pain is in fact a powerful motivator for change. You need to feel a little burn. In fact, when you reach the point of burning desire, there's no fire that can stand in your way.

When you can say "This is important," you're actually saying yes to the obstacle. Everything starts to self-organize once you start to elevate something in importance. Just remember, it's a gift calling you to step forward in a bigger way. Without it, you'd have no puzzle to solve.

You have to want it. Or least surrender to the reality that it must be faced. You must walk through the fire. Gold is often waiting for you on the other side. Your greatest source of untapped power is in the parts of your story that remain unreconciled.

2. Create Bounded Containment

It's natural to want more freedom, options and choices. In particular, creatives and entrepreneurs love the feeling of open possibility. We live for it! Most of our decisions are biased towards freedom and flow and away from constraints and protocols. Which is why it's so easy to avoid the difficult stuff.

Even if you're on a path of freedom, your transformational story needs structure. Just as every canvas has an edge and every map needs a border. You want a boundary to work within and push against. Without a border you can't focus or harness your full energy. You need a container.

That's why it's always easier for people to respond when you present them with a straw-model plan or a beta product. Not vague ruminations or vaporware. You've taken the world of abstract possibilities, and you've reduced it to something specific. You made choices about what matters most and it's reflected in how you organize your story. This choice-making is key to the storytelling process.

Obstacles force you to delineate new boundaries and behaviors. They introduce a natural constraint that you must face or ignore at your peril. This demands that you to create structure! Obstacles are the alchemical fire that will help you make the difficult choices. In the best of circumstances, you feel you have no choice but to respond. It's the ultimate motivational kick in the pants.

3. Find Mentors and Allies

It's impossible to solve most major obstacles all by yourself. That's why you need mentors and allies to help you walk through the fire. The very notion of an obstacle implies something out of your sight and awareness. You can't see it clearly. You didn't see it coming. You don't know what to do about it.

By definition, an obstacle lives outside your sphere of understanding. That's why you want to find your Yoda, your Dumbledore, or even just a gym partner. They'll introduce a fresh perspective and added support, often without the emotional attachments that you bring to the conversation. Remember that your emotions are often what are blurring your vision and ability to confront the obstacle.

As you begin to tackle your problems you may discover an entire constellation of mentors and allies who can help you down the path. Commit to studying the subject you need to solve. Then you'll start to see who you want to model yourself after, who you resonate with, and the mentors will begin to show themselves to you. The old wisdom is true: When the student is ready, the teacher will appear.

Finding your mentors or teachers doesn't mean you won't be working hard and making your own decisions. In fact, the most important thing you cultivate on the hero's journey is self-knowledge. That's the difference between a mentor and a false prophet — one strengthens your self-confidence, the other reinforces their own status and power. A false prophet will dictate to you what the answer should be. A mentor will help you see your options more clearly and empower you to make a more considered and conscious decision.

Seeing the Obstacle as a Gift from the Universe

Obstacles can be our greatest opportunities for character development and business transformation. Often it seems the universe conspires to create a challenging environment, a set of constraints that call on our core essence, our higher purpose, our innate strengths to propel us and our organizations towards a greater destiny.

From a personal health crisis, financial turmoil, losing relevance with your customer base, or questions about who you are as a brand, you're facing your shadow. The obstacles you confront are just antagonistic characters playing their part in the story. They're there working in service to you, advancing the plot, and supporting your transformation. It's all in how you look at it.

CHAPTER THREE

Keep Looking for Solutions

When it comes to losing your keys, or your phone, or your favorite pen, it's true that the one place you'll never look is right under your nose. But when it comes to problems, in life or business, what's right under your nose is usually the only thing you can see. For most of us, that view often looks a lot like a brick wall.

You know the routine. You identify the problem, you define it, outline it, turn it over and over and inside out, and still, it looks like a problem. No solution in sight.

You bang your head against the wall a few times. Then a few more times just to be sure it's a solid wall. No solution, but your headache suggests that wall might be for real.

Why banging your head doesn't break down walls.

Finding a solution requires a different perspective than the one you used to define the problem. It also requires a different brain state. The creative problem-solving activity is a completely different brain function from the analytical problem-defining activity. The wall is not the problem. The real problem is your relationship to the wall. You aren't likely to solve your problem with your nose pressed up against it.

Here are three ways you can move away from the wall and free your mind to identify and create solutions for even the most stubborn of problems.

Get your brain out of problem mode.

Our brains need us to push the reset button. In our office building we have a ping pong table and a quiet corner with a chess board. You might assume that the entrepreneurs whacking at little white balls or furrowing their brows while resting one finger on the bishop's hat aren't as driven as those who are frantically pounding away at their keyboards, but you'd probably be wrong. Ping pong and chess both excite areas of the brain that aid in creativity.

What activities free your creative mind? Is it physical exercise? The stimuli of the outdoors? Maybe you have a drum set you bang on or you play solitaire. Whatever it is, do that. Then take another look at your brick wall, you'll likely see cracks or even big holes that weren't apparent before.

Challenge your programming.

Our brains, much like our computing devices, work on a series of if-then statements. This programming is efficient at keeping the wheels turning when we're barreling along life's highway, but not so effective at navigating crossroads and detours.

What assumptions are you making that might not be true? Probably they were true at one time, maybe as recently as yesterday, but perhaps they aren't true right now. Or maybe it's true that the condition exists, but not true that it cannot be changed. Test everything you believe to be true about your problem and you'll probably find that you are operating on at least one false premise. When you change the "if" the "then" will change as well.

Explore unknown territory.

Chances are, if you are having a problem someone else has experienced the same problem, or at least one similar enough that you can borrow a solution. But the solution may not be in your own backyard. Most innovative problem solvers have become masters of adapting a solution from another application to overcome "impossible" in their own business.

What other business or industry has similar problems? More to the point, what other industry depends on successfully solving that problem in order to survive? How can you adapt their solution to your situation?

Not only will you find inspiration by examining other industries, you'll challenge your brain to connect new dots. By adding unusual elements to the equation you force your brain into creation mode and out of the analytical or overwhelm state you were probably in when you were nose-to-brick with that wall.

While none of these three suggestions will magically solve your problem, they will shift your brain into a state where the solution has a chance of getting through. Because the solution is there, you just have to be in the right brain state to see it.

CHAPTER FOUR

A Secret to Creative Problem Solving

Ever find yourself going over and over a problem in your business, only to hit a dead end or draw a blank?

Find an innovative solution with one simple technique: re-describe the problem.

"The whole idea behind creative problem solving is the assumption that you know something that will help solve this problem, but you're not thinking of it right now," explains Art Markman, cognitive psychologist and author of "Smart Thinking." Put another way, your memory hasn't found the right cue to retrieve the information you need.

Changing the description tells your mind that you're in a different situation, which unlocks a new set of memories. "The more different ways you describe the problem you're trying to solve, the more different things you know about that you will call to mind," says Markman.

Ask yourself two questions:

1. What type of problem is this?

Most of the time, we get stuck on a problem because our focus is too narrow. When you think specifically, you limit your memory and stifle creativity.

Instead, think more abstractly. Find the essence of the problem.

Take vacuum cleaner filters, for example. Vacuums used to have bags that were constantly getting clogged, so innovators focused on how to make a better filter.

James Dyson realized that the problem was actually about separation, or separating the dirt from the air, which doesn't always require a filter. "That freed him to try lots of different methods of separation," says Markman. Hence: the Dual Cyclone vacuum that led Dyson to fame and fortune.

2. Who else has faced this type of problem?

When you think about your problem abstractly, you realize that other people have solved the same type of problem in radically different ways. One of their solutions may hold the key to yours.

For example, Dyson realized sawmills use an industrial cyclone to separate sawdust from air and modified that technology to create the first filter-free vacuum.

"When you begin to realize that the problem you're trying to solve has been solved over and over again by people in other areas, you can look at the solutions they came up with to help you solve your own,".

You may not use one of their solutions exactly, but you free your memory to retrieve more information, making that elusive "aha" moment easier to reach.

By re-describing the problem, you're much more likely to find inspiration for a truly creative innovation.

CHAPTER FIVE

BOOST YOUR CREATIVE POWER

For entrepreneurs, creativity is not simply a luxury. It's an essential survival skill. Common entrepreneurial pitfalls include:

Trying to do everything on your own

Difficulty developing strategies or deciding where to focus your energy

Neglecting to invest in yourself

Falling in love with a venture and pursuing it without proper development

The key to avoiding these traps is understanding how you approach a challenge. The latest creativity research finds we all use our creativity in different ways, but follow a common problem-solving process. Once you understand the creative process, you can intentionally apply it, boosting your creativity and efficiency while strengthening your initiatives. It boils down to these four stages:

Clarify the situation: We explore the issue at hand, find all relevant data that will help us make sense of it and figure out the most effective path to take to resolve it.

Generate ideas: We come up with and select the best new ideas for making a change that best addresses the situation.

Develop solutions: We tinker with those ideas till they are perfect, then break and rebuild them, and then polish them till they shine.

Implement the solution: We put ideas into action by: gaining acceptance of the solution, helping people manage change and adapting solutions as needed.

This process can happen very quickly or deliberately, and in or out of sequence. It can be done in groups or independently. These simple strategies for using the creative process can help keep you on track toward breakthrough success.

1. Stop and think before you start. Self-awareness is a fundamental trait of successful leaders and teams. Once you know your limits, you know where you'll need to bend, where you'll need to ask for help, and where you'll be fine on your own. Thinking about how you get things done, reflecting on the ways your team may work together, will help you be clear about direction and limit the amount of fires you have to put out along the way. This is not "touchy feely" talk. It's serious work that will save you tons of time on the road ahead.

2. Embrace diversity. Knowing how to leverage diversity is a powerful skill. Here we are talking about diversity of thought -- leveraging different ways of thinking. Recognizing where you (and your team) are strong, and where you aren't, is critical. If you know you are not adept at one part of the creative process, seek others who are. Bounce thoughts off them and listen to the new directions their different thinking can provide. Challenge yourself to be open to other's perspectives.

3. Beware of love at first sight. If you find yourself enamored with a particular direction or idea – great, but watch out. You may be onto something, or you may be not exploring things carefully enough. Take the time you need to be sure the direction you are heading fits the need, the idea you have is well thought-out and you're prepared to manage the change effectively.

4. Take one step at a time. Skipping stages can lead to serious problems - like focusing on the wrong issue, or implementing a half-baked solution. We all have preferences for different parts of the process that may lead us to unconsciously gloss-over or completely skip essential steps that would make an innovative idea a reality. Notice where you are in the process and where you need to go next – be deliberate.

5. Know when to move on. When we enjoy a part of the process, we tend to linger in that stage. Witness the guy who spouts a new idea every five minutes, or the gal who keeps asking, "How will this work?" People who apply the process effectively know when their preferences are getting the best of them and are able to shift direction. So don't obsess over endless possibilities or clarifying details. Be sure that you've done a thorough job, you are still on target, and then move on.

Innovation is more than just coming up with a new idea. Instead, it's a process with many components and many players. Any idea, no matter how world-changing, can die in committee or, worse still, after implementation, without attention to all four steps of the creative process. Paying attention to targeting the right issues, developing solutions thoughtfully, and then implementing them with both sensitivity and determination will help you turn that creative spark into a true breakthrough innovation. Knowing the process is like having a good map, now it's up to you to drive innovation home.

CHAPTER SIX

Remember It's All About the Journey

You can change that. The secret of being happy is accepting where you are in life and making the most out of everyday. It doesn't matter how old we are, what we've done, or how much money we have. Our journey is a personal one-full of lessons and reasons to be happy. When we stop comparing ourselves to others and realize how full our lives are, we can appreciate our individual value.

It's important to value the journey, wherever you are in life. Here are some ways to be satisfied-happy, even-with how things are unfolding:

Show gratitude. Find something every single day that you're thankful for. Big or small, it all matters. Tell people how much you appreciate them.

Be committed. Set your goals and stick with them. They made need some adjusting along the way, but you'll keep your eye on the prize.

Cherish your friends. Be around people who love you, not your success. Nurture you relationships and be a true friend without judgment.

Keep on learning. The world is changing rapidly. Whatever your interests, continue to follow them. Or, tackle something new!

Don't multitask. Trying to do more than one thing at once causes burnout and keeps you from focusing on the present.

Balance your life. Easier said than done, but essential. You can't enjoy your age and stage unless you can leave work behind sometimes.

Make family first. Spend time with your family and kids. Go to games and performances. Nothing says I love you more than taking the time to be involved in their lives.

Take time to travel. It opens your mind, makes you more tolerant, and helps you appreciate what you have at home.

Every phase of life has benefits Make the most of where you are today and enjoy the journey because life is short.

CHAPTER SEVEN

FEEL THE FEAR AND DO IT ANYWAY

Sometimes, it feels like success eludes us no matter what we do. We think that if we just got to that next level, things would all work out. But even though we're doing everything right, something just doesn't click.

When that happens, it may be that we unconsciously have a fear of our own success. But why would we be afraid when we're working so hard to be successful? Learn what the fear of success is, what causes it, and how to identify and overcome it.

What is the fear of success?

Fear of success is the concern that once we achieve something new, we'll be incapable of sustaining it or may suffer because of it. Most of the time, we're not consciously aware of this fear. That's because when we focus on a goal, we talk up the positive outcomes of achieving the goal. Rarely do we share with others what might happen when we get to that next level.

Fear of success is not necessarily the fear of reaching that deeply personal achievement unique to each individual. Instead, it is most often the fear of the possible change or consequences of success. It is an anticipation of how others — and oneself — will respond to the triumph. The concern is that achieving success will come at the cost of something else valued in one's life. In many ways, it's similar to the fear of failure.

Sometimes the fear of success can be apparent to a person. Other times it can lie just below the surface, noted in patterns of thought and/or actions repeated by the individual. It takes a high level of self-awareness to identify your own fear of success.

6 ways fear of success shows up in our lives

Fear of success can manifest in different ways. Here are a handful of characteristics to be aware of:

Avoidance

The person may avoid being the center of attention, being praised, or use other avoidance strategies.

Procrastination

The person may delay starting and/or completing a project. As a result of procrastinating, the opportunity may be missed altogether, or the end product may be lackluster.

Perfectionism

The person may believe they are keeping the bar high. But by holding an impossible standard of perfection, the outcome will inevitably be disappointing.

Quitting

The person may find an excuse to quit just before the goal is in sight, over and over again.

Self-sabotage

The person may set obstacles in their own way or stay in unhelpful situations.

Self-destructiveness

At its worst, the fear of success may involve self-destructive behavior. Left unchecked, that derails any real opportunity for success.

How do you identify the fear of success?

Fear of success can manifest in the following symptoms:

Anxiety

The person anticipates the future consequence of their success. Perhaps they worry about being in the spotlight or leaving loved ones behind in pursuit of their success. They might be afraid that success will make things too complicated. They may also worry that critics will talk badly about their work, and that success won't be like anything they imagined.

Guilt

The person may experience a sense of guilt at possibly taking the highest score from someone who held the record for the past ten years. They may be concerned that their light will outshine another who is equally deserving and feel a sense of shame.

Discomfort

People may feel uncomfortable pushing themselves towards goals that still require some growth. This might include anything out of their comfort zone, like public speaking or coming up with their first-ever strategic plan.

Pressure

The person may feel the pressure to have another project in line. They may feel that they have to follow up on this one success with another even better success, and in less time than the first.

Lack of motivation

Sometimes, people who are afraid of success seem lazy, lacking motivation, and having low expectations. Their fear prevents them from ever making progress towards their goals.

Consider the following examples of how fear of success manifests:

The writer who can't stop editing their book, worries about the response of critics, and how they will follow up this book with the next

The woman whose childhood wins served to highlight her brother's losses

The investor who lost large sums of money in a restaurant investment and plays it small, not wanting to "lose it all" again

The entrepreneur who is afraid of growing their business because they doubt whether they can support the growing team year after year

The musician who loves the flow of creating music in private but fears performing the piece in public if he were to receive recognition

8 causes for fear of success

There can be many reasons for a person's fear of success, many of them that have built up over a lifetime:

1. Childhood experience

A childhood experience can negatively impact people on their road to success. If a person had the repeated experience of being taunted for receiving praise in childhood, they might avoid the spotlight. If as a child, their work was never acknowledged or seen as good enough, they might become perfectionists — which is inherently set up for failure.

Childhood experience is deeply ingrained in our neural pathways. The person may expect a negative outcome that has its roots in a playground or sibling experience.

2. Impostor syndrome

A lifetime of self-doubt can lead to a fear that one's achievement will be lacking compared to others. A person may fear not being able to live up to expectations (whether theirs or someone else's) and being found out as an "impostor." Imposter syndrome makes it hard for the person to see that their skill, knowledge, and/or hard work has brought them to the place of accomplishment.

3. Misinterpreting feelings

The feelings of excitement, nervousness, and anxiety result in similar physical responses. A person may interpret one as the other and want to avoid the feeling altogether.

4. Backlash avoidance

People may worry about social repercussions, especially if their success goes against expected norms. A writer may worry about the consequence of their article's cultural critique. Women may be discouraged by the social repercussions of surpassing their male colleagues.

5. Negative experience

An unfavorable outcome to past success may make a person wary of future success. Perhaps collaborators shunned the person for "hogging the limelight." The person may be concerned that future success will mimic that previous response.

6. Poor self-efficacy

The person does not believe that they can achieve the goals they have set for themselves on route to success.

7. Introversion

A person may prefer not to be the center of attention in general. They may shy away from the attention they'll draw to themselves due to the success.

8. Mental health

Clinically diagnosed mental health conditions like post-traumatic stress disorder (PTSD) or generalized anxiety disorder (GAD) can exacerbate the fear of success.

What are the consequences?

Fear of success can hold a person back from achieving their potential — and the accompanying sense of fulfillment in doing so. It can make a person feel stuck and wonder why they feel that way when others around them appear to be flourishing. They may consider what has held them back. Perhaps they take the first step, and then give up when they consider the long road ahead of them. This negatively impacts overall life satisfaction, which affects both personal and professional life. The limiting thoughts result in behaviors that undermine authenticity and satisfaction.

What can you do about it?

If the above sounds like you, consider some of the below approaches to working through your own potential fear of success.

1. Be curious and aware of your thoughts and actions

What are the messages that play over and over in your mind? Is it the cheerleader? The naysayer? The fear-monger? Or all of them at once?

What are your responses to those messages? How do they inform your actions?

2. Start a journal

Journaling can help you track and deeply connect with your thoughts and your response to the world.

In the journal, write:

What is your vision of a life well-lived?

What are your greatest hopes and fears in accomplishing that vision?

What are the best and worst outcomes of achieving success-your life vision? How do you imagine you would respond to both?

3. Reflect

Consider the possible fear of success and how it has shown up for you in the past and present. Do you fear a negative outcome resulting from your success?

4. Acknowledge the fear

By doing so and writing it down, you bring it into the center of your attention.

5. Explore the origins of that fear

Was it something that happened in childhood or adulthood? What message did you take away from your past experiences? What would your life look like if you never pursued this vision of success at all?

Review your journal every week. What are the consistent themes and patterns? By identifying patterns related to success in your thoughts and behaviors, you can begin counteracting them.

Once you identify your negative beliefs and self-talk, you can consider how you can reframe them into generative and empowering beliefs. Sometimes, we can get stuck in our thoughts, so working with a coach can be helpful in creating an alternate response.

6. Visualize success

Visualize yourself being able to navigate both the potential positive and negative outcomes.

7. Self-care

Manage stress and anxiety by taking care of your mind and body. Exercise, eat healthy food, take the time to relax and sleep and enjoy the company of friends and family.

Practice mindfulness and navigate the world with an awareness of how you respond to your circumstances. Deep breathing can give you space to navigate a difficult emotion or thwart a negative, reflexive response when you feel stressed. Focusing on your mental fitness and physical well-being will help you proceed thoughtfully in the world.

8. Self-awareness

Be aware of your discomfort. Sit with the feelings and consider the origin. Is the feeling in service or of disservice to you? How can you adjust your approach?

Be gentle with yourself

The fear of success is very real. With awareness of its impact over time, a person can work to counteract the thoughts and behaviors holding them back and achieve success. The work can be done alone, but often the insights of a coach or therapist can be beneficial in doing the deeper dive. It's not until we start learning from our failures when change happens.

Consider partnering with a coach who can support and challenge you in self-exploration. Once you have uncovered the root of your fear of success together, the coach can help you remain accountable to yourself. They'll cheer you on as you begin to achieve success — and challenge you when old thought patterns and actions rear their ugly head!

If fear of success is causing you distress or disrupting your everyday life, consider seeking the services of a therapist. A therapist familiar with cognitive behavioral therapy (CBT) can assess how negative thought patterns result in maladaptive (unhelpful) behavior. They are trained to work with you to counteract these thoughts with positive ways of thinking and approaching your vision of success. Psychodynamic therapy can help you dive into the unconscious influences of your past. Sometimes, it's something under the surface that hinders our efforts to achieve success.

Remember, it is a life-long journey. Be patient with yourself as you work to unravel the fear, and reconstruct it with a positive expectation of your upcoming success.

CHAPTER EIGHT

ALWAYS ASK PRODUCTIVE QUESTIONS

A successful career and personal life may bring you wealth, prosperity, inner peace, compassion, excitement, freedom and love. No two people have the same exact definition of what success is. If you're looking for ways to achieve your goals, find happiness and advance in your career, it's important to reflect on what this word means to you. In this article, we describe what it means to be successful, and list 24 questions to ask yourself about finding success and happiness in your career and personal life.

What is a successful career and life?

Each person's definition of a successful career and life is unique to their personality, belief system and life experience. For some, a successful career in life is measured by a fulfilling or lucrative career. Others, Feel that a successful life is one that makes a lasting impact on the world or local community. Successful people use their skills, knowledge and positive mindset to set and achieve goals that match their definition of success and happiness.

Here are 24 questions to ask yourself when embarking on a journey to a happy and successful career and life:

1. What does success mean to you?

If your goal is to become successful in your career and life, the first thing you should do is ask yourself what success really means to you. Is it a dollar amount in your bank account or a job title? Or does it mean that you have more freedom or that you work in a place where your ideas are valued.

Knowing what career and personal success look like to you is helpful for developing effective goals regarding your future.

2. What does happiness look like and feel like?

Happiness represents a person's contentment in their lives. Each individual person has their own ideas about what it means to be happy. Ask yourself about the aspects of your life that give you joy and peace. Think about what's happening in those moments and use those memories to help you define what happiness looks like and feels like in your life. Remember that happiness is crucial to success, and working toward inner contentment and personal and career achievements go hand-in-hand.

Related: Employee Happiness: Why It's Important and How To Achieve It

3. Who are your role models for success?

Think about the people who have influenced you over the course of your life. Make a list of the people you know who seem to have successful careers and personal lives. Examine their situations and try to find any commonalities in their work, lifestyles or behaviors that might have lead to their success.

4. Do you have a personal success plan?

A personal success plan is a list of steps or milestones that a person can use to achieve their goals. Having a plan with a projected timeline can help you organize your behaviors and is likely to help you get where you want to go.

5. How do your current responsibilities make you feel?

As you start to visualize what true happiness and success mean for you, it's important to take a moment to assess your current personal and professional circumstances and evaluate how these things make you feel. Getting in touch with your emotions can help you develop your personal success plan.

6. If there were no obstacles in your way, what would you need to do to find success?

It's important to ask yourself this question to help visualize the path to your goals. It will help you to design your success plan and it can motivate you to learn new skills, gain experiences or earn new credentials.

7. What are the main challenges you face in your day-to-day life?

Look at your goals for success and what you believe needs to be done in order to achieve them. It's important to identify financial hurdles, personal obligations or other obstacles you may be facing in your day-to-day life.

Identifying these challenges is the first step in finding the solutions you need.

Related: How To Overcome Challenges in the Workplace

8. Is there anything you could be doing to help navigate those challenges?

Once you identify the primary challenges that may be holding you back from your dreams, it's important to start thinking about ways you might be able to navigate around them. For example, if raising a family is keeping you from earning a degree or credential you need in order to succeed, you may be able to find night classes or a weekend workshop that requires a less significant time commitment than traditional study.

9. Are there any people in your life who you could reach to for help?

A trusted friend, family member or colleague might be able to help you in different ways. For example, you might be able to save money by becoming roommates with a friend, or you could make a plan to arrive to work early each day with a co-worker. Whether to help you ask for is small or large, reaching out to your support system is a great way to help you achieve your goals and find success.

10. What are some things you currently do that contribute to your productivity, happiness and success?

Take some time to note all of the things you currently do that contribute to your productivity, happiness and success. These things may be small or large, and they can be as simple as setting your alarm clock or as big as attending a part-time degree program. Congratulate yourself on these actions and decisions, and make an effort to continue.

11. What time of day are you at your best?

Think about the time of day that you feel most positive and energized. Are you a morning person or evening person, or are you at your best mid-day?

12. What are you doing during this time of day?

Whether you are up and ready to go as the sun rises, or you're more of a night owl, observe your actions, behaviors and feelings during the part of the day that you feel most motivated or positive.

13. Are there any things you can do to capitalize on your most productive time of day?

It's important to try to prioritize your goals during these peak hours, to make as much progress as you can. Consider writing 'to do' lists, setting calendar reminders or blocking out time to complete tasks related to your personal and professional success during that time each day.

Related: 25 Steps To Become a Morning Person

14. How many people count on you on a daily basis?

Whether it's at work, school or at home, take stock in the number of people, or animals, who count on you for small or large things. This exercise can be helpful in motivating you and helping you prioritize your time and energy. It's also helpful for starting to reflect on your need for self-care.

15. Can you schedule some time to recenter or refresh?

Think about your current schedule. Whether you ten free minutes in your day or you can plan to take a day off from work in the near future, it's important to be mindful about re-centering yourself regularly. These moments help people to think about their goals, and they may even help people to become happier. Here are eight ways to refresh or recenter your thoughts and energy throughout your day:

Take a walk in nature.

Spend time with a friend.

Meditate or complete a breathing exercise.

Take a refreshing shower.

Do something spirited or silly, like a cartwheel.

Call a family member or loved one.

Offer someone you care about a hug.

Paint, draw or do something creative.

16. Do your regular practices give you time to grow and learn in your industry?

Take mental inventory of your daily schedule and regular routines. Think about the moments you have available in your day that you may be able to dedicate fifteen or twenty minutes to your goals. You can read a chapter in an industry related book, or you can read an article or watch a video related to learning new skills.

17. Does your daily routine promote your health, well-ness and happiness?

When trying to better yourself and advance in your career, it's crucial to take time to care for your personal well-being. Here are 10 tips to consider for wellness a healthy self-care regimen:

Aim to get between six and nine hours of rest each night.

Hydrate and eat balance meals with plenty of fresh fruits and vegetables.

Make efforts to relax or unwind at least once a day.

Practice healthy hygiene habits.

Engage in an enjoyable leisure activity at least once a week.

Spend time with friends, family or pets.

Plan to take an occasional day off from work.

When possible, complete a light physical exercise at least two times per week.

Connect with your doctors when needed.

Enjoy the sunshine or fresh air when possible.

Related: 10 Benefits of Wellness Programs in the Workplace

18. After reviewing your answers, what are the top three to five things you'd like to prioritize in your daily life?

This question is important for self-reflection. Making honest assessments about your daily behaviors can help you to improve your habits and become healthier and happier. Happiness and health go hand-in-hand with success.

19. After thinking about these questions, do you have any new short-term or long term-goals regarding your success and happiness?

This question is important for helping you prioritize and achieve your goals. Focusing on a few goals, instead of trying to change every aspect of your life all at once, makes goal-setting more reasonable and attainable.

20. Would a schedule to help you stay on track?

If you think that a schedule or daily list might help you organize your routines and manage your goals, set aside time to create one. A spread sheet, e-calender or old-fashioned piece of paper can be all you need to stay motivated, organized on track to success.

21. Are there ways to make yourself accountable for meeting your goals?

Think about ways to help yourself stay accountable for the plans and schedules you've made. You may want to write your thoughts and post them in a place that's highly visible, like your kitchen fridge or near your mirror. Or, you might try asking someone to partner with you in your new routine.

Related: The Difference Between Accountability and Responsibility

22. How do you handle setbacks?

On the road to success, you may encounter some challenges. Analyze the way you's handled setbacks in the past. Thinking about this step proactively can help you plan to stay positive and driven if an unforeseen obstacle arises.

23. What motivates you and incentivizes you when you have a goal?

Some people are motivated by regular small rewards, like tasty treats or spending a night in with a friend—while others find larger and less regular rewards, like taking a vacation, to be more motivating. When trying to lead the most successful life you can, it's important to make a plan and set a schedule. Using rewards or reward systems to help motivate you when you have a goal is crucial to sticking to your plan and finding success.

24. Do you currently use any strategies for staying positive?

A positive mindset can help you stay focused and motivated when setting your sights toward success. Here are five strategies for staying positive:

Use positive words of affirmation to start or end your day.

Express gratitude for those around you.

Give yourself feedback or small rewards when you do something well.

Share your success stories with gay people you care about.

Treat each day as an opportunity to succeed.

CHAPTER NINE

Understand the Best Waste of Energy Is Complaining

You possess the power to create the business and life you want. You won't fully realize that power, however, if you spend time focusing on the negative thoughts that doom so many entrepreneurs. And you certainly won't succeed if you think it's okay to vocalize your worries, internally or externally, by complaining.

The tricky part about complaining is that most of the time it's about something that might be true. "I don't have enough funding." "Our product launch is delayed." "Things aren't moving fast enough." Even though these statements might be true, people don't want to hear complaints -- and complaints won't help you find a solution.

I know complaining well. In my mid-twenties, I complained so much my brother had to call me out. I'm glad he did, because it sparked a process of exploring why I complained and how to fix it. This article contains the results of that effort so you don't need to go through the whole process yourself.

Here are seven daily habits that helped me to stop complaining and to start attracting more happiness, fulfillment and success in my life.

1. Watch uplifting videos

I regularly watch or listen to videos and talks that uplift me, and remind me of my creative power and the Law of Attraction. I watch videos from Jim

Carrey, Alan Watts, Kute Blackson, Abraham Hicks, Oprah and many more.

Tap into the power of positive thinking by consuming content that shifts you from a victim mindset to a creator mindset. And it's so easy. You can download videos from off Youtube, listen to podcasts, and use the TED app to download talks to your smartphone.

2. Be nice to yourself

Rather than creating and trapping yourself in a negative reality with habitual complaining, find ways to treat yourself well. Say nice things to yourself instead of hurtful and limiting self-talk. Get massages, relax with a good book or friends, go get your nails done, or plan a weekend getaway. Take time to reward yourself just for being you.

3. Use the power of intention

State and repeat a written intention to stop complaining and make it part of your daily awareness. Use a mantra that focuses on the positive, such as "I am anticipating a pleasant surprise." What we focus on expands, so keep your intention front of mind. It also helps to meditate on this mantra so you can really feel it.

4. Keep a gratitude journal

One hack that has changed my life is the nighttime habit of writing down three things I was grateful for that day. Your sources of gratitude may be profound, such as closing a big business deal, or simply a bright spot in your day. If you can't think of anything, write that you are alive, you have shelter and you have food. That's more than many people can say.

5. Tell others about your goal

Let the people closest to you know that you want to stop being negative. Ask for their help with building awareness by having them tell you when you complain. My brother and roommates really helped me with this. You'll probably find that your friends will be excited to help.

6. Take up a new sport or activity

I've noticed that I tend to complain more frequently when I feel stagnated or bored. There's a fun remedy that will help you feel empowered again: learn something new.

It can be anything you are curious about or enjoy. Learn a new language. Take dancing lessons. Do yoga. The act of learning, progressing and achieving will bring excitement and empowerment to your life. I took up surfing and boxing, and it worked well for me.

7. Go out and play

Somewhere along the path to adulthood, we lose touch with our child-like and natural inclination to "play." Playing can be anything that you find fun. Go camping and hunt for sticks to roast s'mores, spend time with friends, or just goof around. You can accelerate this feeling by getting down on the floor and playing with your kids, nieces and nephews.

Final word

Complaining is a negative habit that affects us mentally, emotionally and physically. By turning to some simple daily practices, you can rid yourself of this self-defeating habit - and watch the world around you change.

CHAPTER TEN

Don't Play the Blame Game

Finding Solutions, Not Fault

Imagine you're heading up an important project. The deadline is looming, but the work is going to be delayed and your boss wants to know why.

You and your team are asked to explain yourselves and, before you know it, the "blame game" begins. The discussion goes round in circles as you try to figure out who's at fault, and why.

Wasting time pointing fingers, rather than looking for solutions, is a common occurrence but it's far from constructive.

In this article, we explore what the blame game is, how to stop it once it's started, and how you can avoid it in the first place.

What Is the Blame Game?

When something goes wrong and we feel threatened, it's natural to want to defend ourselves against any repercussions. We might find ourselves scapegoating or trying to shift the blame elsewhere.

We may try to distance ourselves from a problem, fearing that taking responsibility for errors or mistakes could harm our careers or make us look bad.

But this approach doesn't solve anything. Shifting the blame won't help you to meet that deadline, and it doesn't fix the problem that caused the delay.

Sometimes it's all too obvious when a team is playing a blame game. But it can happen in more subtle ways, too.

Here are some warning signs to watch out for:

Exclusion: one or two people in the team are regularly excluded or marginalized. They may be "weaker" than the others (either in character or position), or absent from the discussion.

"Finger pointing": team members find fault within the group. For example, "Jack was supposed to check those figures before the presentation."

Denial: people deny responsibility or come up with excuses. They may make comments such as, "That's nothing to do with me, no one showed that information to me!"

Negativity: no solution is identified to fix the issue at hand. Instead, people become fixated on finding fault. They struggle to move forward and only focus on the negative.

The Impact of Blame

Blaming others can have a detrimental effect on morale and performance. Team members may feel belittled or humiliated if they're pinpointed for blame – especially if it's not their fault.

A culture of blame may also lead to individuals or teams being scapegoated when the real problem may lie elsewhere, or have a number of causes. It's easier to blame someone in another department or building than it is to point the finger at someone you sit with every day.

Over time, this type of scapegoating may even perpetuate bias or prejudice, or lead to accusations of discrimination . Also, it can damage the integrity of other team members who witness it, especially if they do nothing to stop it.

"Passing the buck" can deplete trust with customers and suppliers, and give your organization a bad name. Conversations along the lines of, "Well, that's the finance team's fault, not ours, so I can't help you" can make the whole company seem incompetent.

Blame can also stunt creativity and innovation within your organization – if people are afraid to try new things in case they don't work out, this can reduce team and company performance in the longer term.

Finally, some individuals may be prone to accepting blame where it is not warranted. A protective manager, for example, may "take the rap" for someone else's mistake. Or, an individual who's highly self-critical may view everything as their fault, even when it isn't.

CHAPTER ELEVEN

Maximize Your Strengths

Strengths and superheroes: Growing up, we are introduced to several superheroes which we often idolize, even as we grow older. We tend to imitate them too and imagine all kinds of scenarios. As adults, however, we somehow choose to ignore this imagination, and that's our biggest mistake. Why not turning your imagination into reality? Why not be your own superhero and learn how to be successful with the way you are?

Every person has their own talents and skills. To help you find out the things that you are good at and that would make you successful, here are 5 easy steps to maximize your strengths.

1. Clarify your known strengths

There are actually two types of strengths – the known (realized) and the unknown (unrealized) strengths. Both of them are something that we are good at and give us energy to keep going. These strengths are often mistaken with the "learned behaviors", which are the things that we are good at but drain our energy. Learned behaviors are like weaknesses, they also de-energize our mind and body even if we are good at doing them.

The Strengths Model

By clarifying our realized strengths versus the learned behaviors we will be able to maximize the use of our energy. If we will also be able to identify and discover our unrealized strengths and find opportunities to use them, we will feel more motivated and be more likely to achieve success.

2. Identify your hidden strengths

The acronym SIGN helps people to easily identify their strengths.

Success (Your strength is something that makes you feel successful.)

Instinct (It is something natural – a thing that you can't help but be drawn to.)

Growth (In this area, you grow, nurture and develop into a better you.)

Need (It is something that fills your innate needs.)

Answering these questions will also help you know your passion and strengths:

What are you good at?

What do you enjoy doing?

What gives you energy or motivates you?

3. Work out how to use your strengths more

In maximizing your strengths, you can use the acronym BEST as a guide.

Be clear – Identify your strengths and where and when to use them.

Examine – How can you apply your strengths better?

Specialize – Focus on your specialty strengths and learn to improve them.

Transfer – Share your strength with others. In sharing you will find out the areas you are missing and be able to work on them more.

4. Avoid your weaknesses and moderate the use of your "learned behaviors"

If you focus on what you are not good at and what you can't do, you're just wasting your time. Overusing your learned behaviors, on the other hand, will just make you de-motivated and exhausted. Learn how to avoid weaknesses and control the use of your learned behaviors to take full advantage of your strengths.

5. Beware of overdone strengths

There is a big difference between great attention to detail and being obsessive, as well as being confident and being arrogant. Overdone strengths often result in the very opposite of what you are expecting. These can even ruin your credibility. So, how are you able to get rid of overdone strengths? Here are some useful tips.

Be aware of how you act when you're stressed or nervous.

Learn relaxation techniques.

Work out how to use additional strengths in stressful situations.

Success is affected by how you are able to manage your weaknesses. But, it is a lot more about how you are able to maximize both your known and unknown strengths.

Identifying your strengths and building your life based on them are essential for success. Without knowing how to recognize your strengths and maximize them, you may waste a lot of time doing the wrong things. Can you imagine spending years of hard work only to realize at the end that you have poured your time and energy (not to mention money) into the wrong things?

That's why I believe these 12 lessons on maximizing your personal strengths are important. I summarized these lessons from the book Now, Discover Your Strengths by Marcus Buckingham and Donald O. Clifton. Rather than writing a review of the book, I'll directly give you the gems in the form of these 12 lessons.

First of all, let's be clear about the definition of strength used here: a strength is consistent near perfect performance in an activity. You have strength in something if you consistently achieve near perfect performance in it. This definition is important to bear in mind, as we go through the lessons.

So here are the 12 essential lessons to maximize your personal strengths:

1. Focus on your strengths, not your weaknesses

You will excel only by maximizing your strengths, never by fixing your weaknesses. Capitalize on your strengths, and manage around your weaknesses. Managing around your weaknesses will free you up to hone your strengths to a sharper point.

2. An ability is a strength only if you can fathom yourself doing it repeatedly, happily, and successfully

Besides consistently performing it successfully, you should also derive some intrinsic satisfaction from the activity.

3. Organize your life around your strengths

Organize your life around your strengths so that these strengths can be applied. Find or carve out a role that draws on these strengths every day. This will make your life more productive and fulfilled.

4. There are three raw materials of strengths: talents, knowledge, and skills

Talents are your naturally recurring patterns of thought, feeling, or behavior (more in lesson #6).

Knowledge consists of the facts and lessons learned (more in lesson #7).

Skills are the steps of an activity (more in lesson #8).

It is the combination of talents, knowledge, and skills that creates your strengths.

5. The most important of the three raw materials are talents

Talents are the most important because they are innate whereas skills and knowledge can be acquired through learning and practice.

6. Your talents are enduring because they are somehow "hardwired" into your brain

Basically, your talents are the strongest synaptic connections in your brain. It is the path of "least resistance" in your brain which makes you naturally tend to go that way.

7. There are two kinds of knowledge: factual and experiential

Factual knowledge is content. For example, when you start to learn a language, factual knowledge is the vocabulary. Factual knowledge won't guarantee excellence, but excellence is impossible without it. It gets you into the game.

Experiential knowledge is the knowledge that can be acquired only through experiences. It teaches you what works and what doesn't. It cannot be taught in classrooms. Instead, it's something that you must discipline yourself to pick up along the way and retain.

To build your strengths, you need both kinds of knowledge.

8. Skills bring structure to experiential knowledge

A skill basically is the formulation of all the accumulated knowledge into a sequence of steps that, if followed, will lead to performance – not necessarily great performance but at least acceptable performance.

It enables you to avoid trial and error and incorporate the best discoveries directly into your performance. A skill is designed to make the secrets of the best easily transferable.

9. The key to building your strength is to identify your dominant talents and then refine them with knowledge and skills

It's essential to understand how to distinguish your natural talents from things you can learn. The first thing you should do is identifying your natural talents. After that, you should acquire the required knowledge and skills to refine your talents.

10. Practice doesn't (necessarily) make you perfect

You can't reach near perfect performance in any activity you choose just by practicing. It also requires certain natural talents. While you can always improve your performance with practice, it might not take you to consistent near perfect performance. Unless you have the necessary talent, your improvements will be modest.

11. A sure way to identify your talents is stepping back and watching yourself for a while.

Watch yourself for a while when you try an activity. See how quickly you pick it up. See whether you become absorbed in the activity to such an extent that you lose track of time.

12. There are four clues to help you identify your talents

More specifically, look for these four clues to identify your talents:

Spontaneous reactions

What are your spontaneous, top-of-mind reactions to the situations you encounter? These top-of-mind reactions provide the best trace of your talents because they show where the paths of "least resistance" in your brain are.

For example, when you hear that your employee cannot come because his child is sick, what is your first reaction? If your first reaction focuses on the ill child because you care about her, you may have a talent of empathy.

Yearnings

Your strongest connections are irresistible. They exert a magnetic influence, drawing you back time and again. These stronger connections will keep calling out to you, demanding to be heard. If you want to discover your talents, you should pay them heed.

Rapid learning

The speed at which you learn a new skill provides a telltale clue to the talent's presence and power. Whatever the skill is, if you learned it rapidly, your talents may be at work.

Satisfactions

Your strongest synaptic connections are designed so that when you use them, it feels good. So, if it feels good when you perform an activity, chances are that you are using a talent.

Having read all the lessons, there are two questions you should ask yourself:

Do I currently build my career on top of my talents?

Have I organized my life around my strengths?

If your answer to any of these questions is no, you'd better take action before it's too late.

CHAPTER TWELVE

BE IN IT TO WIN IT

You Gotta Be In It To Win It

Why you should stop the self-reject and go after your dreams.

What are you forfeiting because you're saying "No" to yourself? What streams of opportunities are passing you by because you seemed to have got it figured out that you can't have them? Why bother trying since your effort is doomed to failure?

You want the job but you already figured out that you'll be rejected if you apply, so you declined?

You want to write the book, but you already figured out nobody will read it except, of course, your octogenarian grandmother, who doesn't have much else to do with her time?

You want to get the raise, but you figured out already that the answer would be no, so you don't bother to ask?

You want to write for that publication but you've already convinced yourself that it's is for writers better than you. As for you, your ideas are rubbish and your writing, horrible.

You've toned down and resigned to a lesser ambition as you've got it perfectly figured out that someone so ordinary as you is not worthy of any high aspiration?

These are various manifestation of self-rejection.

Saying No to yourself. Denying you ever nourished the dream just because you think you've figured out that you can't have it.

Self-rejection feels safe for a while, until.

Self rejection feels harmless, safe even cozy. Until, that is, you discover the ever growing mountain of regret building up around you. Until you find yourself sat there wondering what could have been if you had dared to take the chance?

Could you have gotten the job?

Could you have gotten the admission? The scholarship?

Could what is gathering dust on your hard drive have been a bestseller? Could it have been a story that will set someone's soul alight?

Could you have gotten the raise?

Could you have made a difference if you had given the encouragement anyway?

We make the mistake all the time.We say No to ourselves. We park out dreams. We fail to go for it.

When we say No to ourselves before we hear it from the world, we know we've got at least one possibility ruled out: we won't get to hear it from the world.

Because that stings.

It hurts.

It hurts to get the email, "your application was unsuccessful this time".

It hurts to hear your boss turn down your request for promotion.

It hurts to release your 40,000-word tome to the world laden with grand expectation to only two sales in 4 months—one from your close friend out of pity for your hard work and the other from your sister, for roughly the same reason. Yikes.

If you tell yourself No before any of these scenario could happens at least you can feel safe for a while. You get to avoid the pain of rejection, the pain of failure, of falling flat on your face.

But what happens when, sooner or later, you're forced to deal face to face with the pain of regret gnawing at your soul? The pain of what could have been?

Self-rejection is Just a Symptom

Self-rejection is the indicator that you have given the fear of failure an out-sized importance. You have become so scared of failing at something — at anything — that you self-reject, a fancy way of saying you decide not to try at all.

You allow the fear of failure to wrap up in its claws till you begin to undermine your own efforts— subconsciously—to ward off the possibility of a larger failure.

When you fear failure so much, it makes doing nothing more attractive and therefore you resist moving forward. You miss great opportunities.

But here's something you must get. It's not nicety but its true.

If you are not folding your arms hoping the wind of fortune blow in your favour, if you go out and go after what you want, if you go chasing your dreams, putting your time, effort, energy into achieving something worthwhile, then it's as close as to a guarantee as you can get:

You'll get rejected a lot. You'll fail a lot.

Your ideas will be rejected, your efforts, your offers, your writing, your application, your prose, your essay, your appeal, etc, will be deemed not-worthy.

See, Rejecters are everywhere—some lurking, some in plain sight: agents, editors, reviewers, award-givers, readers, your boss, admission board, scholarship board, curators...name them.

You have to be cool with that.

You have to see the reality that those who succeed a lot also fail a lot. "The master has failed more times than the beginner has even tried." is how Stephen McCranie succinctly put it.

What you should not do — or stop doing — is self-rejecting.

Yes, rejection is painful but it's a risk we must take — and one worth taking. The alternative is living with the bucketloads of regrets and missed opportunities.

You can recognize that getting punched in the face just comes with the territory. If you get in the ring you'll (more than likely) get punched in the face. You can decide to roll with the punches and carry on fighting. And you might, who knows, get to a point where you get rejected—just like several before—but it doesn't elicit the same visceral reaction it used to. And, you, my friend, are growing.

What Are The Odds?

The question we often ask is what are the chances?

And it's a very good question to ask. You want to know what you're giving your time, your energy, your resources to. You want to know if you're not wasting a bullet. Makes perfect sense.

But the answer often is: it's hard to tell.

It's hard to know if that job application is the one that will land your dream job.

It's hard to know if that next business will be a successes or a failure.

It's hard to know if that next article is the one that will go crazily viral.

But you know what's easier to know?

It is that if you don't make the attempt, the odds quickly tumbles to zero.

Think about that.

"If you don't go after what you want, you'll never have it. If you don't ask, the answer is always no. If you don't step forward you're always in the same place."

Here's the one thing that's abundantly clear, above all else:

You gotta be in it to win it.

So, stop the self-reject and go after your dreams. Start today.

If you found this post helpful, you'll also enjoy my INSPIRATION PALACE newsletter. It is a weekly collection of my best writings to inspire you and help you get better at work and life. Subscribe here.

CHAPTER THIRTEEN

KNOW THAT SUCCESS ATTRACTS SUCCESS

Attract Success by Living Life to the Fullest. There's a vast, fantastic world out there. Foster your curiosity, and it will lead you to amazing places.

Read.

Ferociously. Everything you can get your hands. Join a book club. Imbibe books about personal development, communication, achievement, biographies, leadership, success, marketing, sales, business, entrepreneurship. You'll do many things you may regret, but you will never ever regret spending time reading. Good sources of reading lists are Quora, blogs (Google 10 best books for …), Amazon (look for recommendations in categories, popular books with high ratings).

2. Accept uncertainty.

This comes from The Seven Spiritual Laws of Success: A Practical Guide to the Fulfillment of Your Dreams: Deepak Chopra, a must-read for getting started out. There's uncertainty to everything; the sooner you can embrace that, the sooner you'll be able to leverage it. "You must give up the life you have planned in order to have the life that is waiting for you." --Joseph Campbell

3. Agree.

With everything and everyone. Stop arguing, stop trying to control every scenario, stop trying to prove yourself right. You'll never change anyone's opinion through argument, and no one will remember if you're right. Seek consensus. Groups, teams, and life move much better when harmonized than with discord.

4. Be curious.

There's a vast, fantastic world out there. Foster your curiosity, and it will lead you to amazing places.

5. Be open minded.

Your opinions will change drastically on many, many things. The opinions you hold with absolute conviction may be very different in a few years. Don't let those opinions get in the way of meeting people and experiencing things.

6. Learn from adversity.

You'll experience challenges and adversity you can't imagine right now. You'll have a choice when you have one of these experiences: Either see it as an obstacle or focus on what you can learn and how you can grow from the experience. It won't be easy, but choose the later relentlessly, and you'll grow in ways you can never imagine.

7. Foster the growth mindset.

Watch this: The power of belief -- mindset and success

8. Get out of your comfort zone.

It sounds cliched, but it's true. If you stay within your limits, you'll never know what you're capable of.

9. Don't hold onto the wrong things.

Grudges, anger, opinions. Let them go, quickly.

10. Travel.

Get out and explore. Another thing you will never ever regret. Go places you'd never think you'd go. Max out your vacation time every year. Take a few weeks off between jobs and travel. Save up for a year and take a few months off.

11. Don't wait for the right time or the right thing to say.

For anything. Most of the time if you wait for the right time, you'll be too late. Those who win in the world are the ones who speak up and take immediate action. You might say a few things you later regret, but you'll regret not saying anything more.

12. Don't look for the perfect scenarios, partner, or job.

Everyone sees success and wonders how Jobs and Wozniak found each other, the perfect partners. Well, it wasn't the one-in-a-billion odds that they found each other; they made each other the perfect partners, pushed each other's knowledge and expertise, and built Apple on their collective knowledge and energy. The vision of your career might include a high-profile company or opportunity (e.g. work at Google, live in San Francisco), but don't get hung up on these. Focus on the motivation behind that scenario rather than that goal.

13. Provide value in the world.

Money and success are common goals, but so many people often don't achieve these in spite of their being nearly universal goals. Money and success are important, but focus on creating value in the world first. The biggest disrupters didn't do it because it would lead to money or fame. They did it because they wanted to change things. They saw a different future and created that. Look at Facebook. Mark Zuckerberg built a tool for Harvard students originally. It now has over 1.4 billion users! Wake up and think about what you can do to create value in the world to your friends and family, your company, your co-workers, your country.

This question originally appeared on Quora. Ask a question, get a great answer. Learn from experts and access insider knowledge. You can follow Quora on Twitter, Facebook, and Google+. More questions:

Young Adults: What are examples of assumptions that people passionately believe in when they are young that turn out to be false?

Life Lessons: How can I make my life simpler?

Career Advice: What are a few unique pieces of career advice that nobody ever mentions?

Success doesn't happen "to" you. It happens because of you.

In the words of Napoleon Hill, "Success comes to those who are success-conscious." If you make progress your most important goal and actively make strides to improve, you will begin to attract success like a magnet.

During my first 4 years of blogging, I pitched guest posts to every website. I emailed every influencer. I tweeted every writer. I hand-wrote letters to authors and asked if they would mentor me.

Maybe 5% ever responded — most of which were thanks-but-no-thanks rejections.

But finally, I started taking myself and my writing extremely seriously. I stopped emailing websites hoping people would say yes and just focused on building something people could no longer ignore.

I began attracting enormous success when I made PROGRESS my biggest goal.

I finally stopped chasing success. I knew the more I improved, the more success I would attract; success would take care of itself.

These easy habits you can start today that will make you automatically attract enormous success.

Label Every Obstacle as a Learning Opportunity

Most people only see obstacles as unfortunate problems that prevent them from progress. They run into some difficulties, throw up their hands, and go home.

The world's most successful people automatically attract enormous success by using their obstacles as a distinct, unique advantage. Whatever obstacles arise are immediately embraced as an opportunity to learn and grow.

This implacable attitude confounds most other people, and always attracts significant success over time.

People who automatically attract enormous success do so by making every obstacle an opportunity.

Most people view problems in a negative light, or at best, with resigned duty. Few people see obstacles for what they really are — incredibly potent, powerful fuel to teach you new skills that make you better.

If you want to automatically attract enormous success, see every problem as an opportunity to learn.

"The struggle against an obstacle inevitably propels the fighter to a new level of functioning."

This is how you bend success to your will. For you, the harder the obstacle, the greater the victory. The more difficult the problem, the more you'll learn and grow.

The world loves people with this mindset. Individuals with this attitude inspire faith, confidence, and trust in others.

Teach Yourself the Skills You Never Thought You Could Learn

Most people don't know how to:

Self-publish an eBook

Start a blog

Create their own podcast

Design their own online course

Consistently wake up at 5AM

I didn't believe I could do any of these things. But I've taught myself each of these skills — and evolved into a much better version of myself in the process.

I have a degree in English. I've been writing for eight years; I blog, I create content. "I'm only a writer," I would tell myself. "I don't do tech stuff."

But after a mind-numbing week of going back-and-forth with perplexing tech support, I realized I had recoded my entire website and created my first online course from scratch. It was like looking up from the hood of your car and realizing you, a complete amateur, had just replaced the transmission by yourself.

Most people have an extremely limiting mindset of themselves. Some even wear these limitations as a backwards badge of honor:

"Oh, I have no idea how to write a book."

"I'm awful at all that creative stuff."

"I can't start a podcast, I wouldn't know where to start."

"I couldn't start my own business, I'd be a terrible businessman."

This disbelief is negative power. As Joseph Murphy wrote in The Power of Your Subconscious Mind, "Your subconscious mind will accept any suggestions, however false, and responds according to the nature of the suggestion given."

What you tell yourself becomes true.

Want to automatically attract enormous success? Teach yourself some new tricks. You increase your scope of influence, your ability to converse with experts in different fields, and most importantly, your self-belief.

Learning the skills you always thought you couldn't learn destroys the self-doubt and fear that prevents so many people from ever achieving greatness.

Be Prepared For Every Possible Opportunity

Extraordinary, life-changing opportunities pass by unsuspecting people every day.

Most people are unprepared and ill-equipped to seize a huge opportunity. Since they have accepted too many mediocre obligations, they have neither the means nor the eye to recognize truly great opportunities.

Top-quality opportunities will not wait for you. If you are not ready, they'll pass you by and find someone else a minute later.

The magic is, once you begin seizing opportunities as they come, more opportunities will gravitate to you. The more you capitalize on, the more come your way.

Most people are simply too prideful to learn new skills — they think learning how to code is irrelevant, or that mastering new online tools should be done by someone else.

In today's world, the success doesn't go to the luckiest or smartest — it goes to the hungriest.

Prepare yourself. Commit to learning and creating, not entertainment and distraction.

Life-changing opportunities will come, and you must be ready to seize them when no one else is.

BONUS

For every day you keep going, thousands of others quit.

Often, success comes at the end — to those who are still there after everyone else has left. It's like compound interest, where the largest gains come after much time has passed.

Most people quit before they even get a chance to succeed. They try something for a few weeks, even a few months; but before they reach a place of automatically attracting success, they give up and go home.

CHAPTER FOURTEEN

ACTUALLY CHOOSE TO BE SUCCESSFUL

So, you want to finally discover how to be successful?

First, imagine where you'll honestly be in the next five years.

Maybe on a beach, working remote while drinking your favorite cocktail or beer. Or maybe you'll be sitting on a couch, watching Netflix, and still dreaming.

Your success lies in your hands.

I could tell you all the things you need to do to be successful, and at first you'll probably do a couple of those things, but six months from now you'll be back to your current routine.

So, do you want to finally figure out how to be successful and do it. Or do you want to keep dreaming about it?

If you're serious about becoming successful, keep reading.

Want to start your path to to success with your own business? Find cool products to sell on Handshake, your wholesale one-stop shop.

What is Success in Life?

Success in life is whatever you define it to be. Maybe for you, you want to determine how to be successful to achieve financial freedom or a flexible work schedule.

Some may want to travel the world while others just want to pursue what they're passionate about.

Being successful isn't necessarily about being rich or winning awards, it can be also about personal fulfillment.

If you had to design your perfect day, what would it look like?

Would you be sitting on a bench next to a lake writing your memoir? Do you imagine yourself climbing Mount Kilimanjaro and taking that big, deep breath once you get to the top? Or maybe you just want to spend an entire day playing with your kids?

Why you want to learn how to be successful in life will be personal to you. Your partner, parents, and friends may have their own definition of success. But their definitions aren't for you.

Whatever it is that'll make you feel fulfilled and happy is what you need to focus on while mastering the art of becoming a success.

Importance of Success

Most people obsess over how to be successful because we all want to feel like we matter.

Without achieving any success, we might look back on our life disappointed by our lack of impact on the world.

Striving to achieve a greater purpose is what keeps us fighting to survive and grow.

While you might not become an international success, your life can still have an impact on others.

The goal of achieving success will help you live a more purposeful life by pushing you to overcome obstacles, work a bit harder and pursue happiness.

How Can I Become Successful?

Truth is, you'll probably never become successful.

I'm not saying this to be a jerk, I'm saying it because the odds are stacked against you.

On the bright side, it's never been easier to learn how to be successful. There's never been more millionaires in the world than there are today.

Also, I'm kind of hoping that by telling you you'll never be successful that you'll think to yourself, 'Man, this Nicole girl is kind of a jerk. I want to prove her wrong just so I can leave a nasty comment telling her a few months from now that she was SO wrong about me.'

Do it. Prove me wrong!

In my career, I've found having a chip on my shoulder and being angry at the world has resulted in me growing at a faster rate than everyone else.

I like to pretend that I'm the biggest failure in the world with everything to prove.

If someone doubts me, I do whatever it takes to prove them wrong.

Like I always say, 'Don't piss me off, because when I'm angry I'll always win.'

But truth is, I secretly love it when people diss me.

Truth is, you'll probably never become successful.

I'm not saying this to be a jerk, I'm saying it because the odds are stacked against you.

On the bright side, it's never been easier to learn how to be successful. There's never been more millionaires in the world than there are today.

What Does It Take To Be Successful?

Nothing will motivate you better than a fuming rage deep inside you.

So, here's your diss: You spend way too much time on unimportant tasks while pretending that you're 'researching or learning or finding motivation.' But truth is, you're slacking. And you're never going to get your act together unless you START WORKING. So, if you want to be able to pay your bills or travel the world, it's not going to happen if you never take that first step.

How to Be Successful in Life – 8 Ways to Be Successful in Life

#1. Stop Looking for the Silver Bullet

The silver bullet is that you need to put in the work everyday for years.

It's not some Facebook ads hack. Or some magical $2000 conference.

But no matter how many times people tell you that, you're still going to dig around for the secret answer.

Why?

Because you don't want to put in the work.

You want to be an overnight success.

Not gonna happen, though.

So if I were you, I'd start creating.

#2. Start Creating Better Goals

'My goal is to make a ton of money.'

And you're wondering why you still haven't made it.

Your goal isn't actionable.

And quite frankly it isn't that motivating either.

Money is great and all but it won't leave you fulfilled.

What's your big life purpose?

Maybe being successful to you means taking action to clean the world's oceans or to help prevent animals from becoming extinct.

Now, how do you do that?

Well, you need money, and that's where your money goal comes into play.

How much money do you need to help solve those problems.

Get a calculator, reach out to some nonprofits and start crunching numbers.

Then, use that exact number as your goal.

And add an exact date to it.

'I want to make $103,476.37 by December 31st, 2021 to invest in cleaning the world's oceans so we can preserve ocean life and have clean drinking water.'

Now you've got a specific goal, a date to achieve it by and a purpose for achieving it.

#3. Stop Looking for Validation

If you're looking for ways to be successful in life, you're not going to find it in the people around you. Unless, everyone around you is a giant success.

Your mom, dad, best friend, partner, and dog don't need to approve your business ideas.

Live life your way. Stop looking to others for validation that you're on the right track.

Wanna know how you're on the right track?

When you ask yourself, 'Am I living the life I want?'

If the answer is yes, you're on the right track.

If the answer is no, you've got some changes to make.

Don't let outsiders cloud your thinking.

People always think they know what's best for you.

But only you'd know what that is.

Trust yourself a bit more and you'll realize you know what you're doing.

#4. Start Living Your Dreams

Being successful in life isn't about a magical moment when everything falls into place.

It's about the little moments in between.

Moments where you're happy. Moments that you're really soaking in.

Truth is, you can experience those moments even if you're currently stuck in a 9 to 5.

If your goal is to run an online business, you've got evenings and weekends where you can start plugging away.

Maybe you want to be a digital nomad, you can talk to your boss about working remote for three weeks while you work abroad.

I know what you're thinking, you want it all and you want it now.

But truth is, unless you take those baby steps, you won't really know whether it's something you want or something you think you want.

You can still start trying to figure out a plan on how to be successful whether you're at a 9 to 5 or not.

I'm not saying stay at your 9 to 5 if you're miserable. I'm just saying that the 9 to 5 on its own isn't always the only cause of your frustration or unhappiness.

#5. Stop Looking for a Mentor

There's nothing wrong with mentorship. It can actually be really great for building your career.

Most people don't want mentorship though, they want someone to do all the work for them.

Entrepreneurship and being successful is all about taking ownership.

You talk a big game about wanting freedom, but when it comes to designing your first store, you ask for so much feedback.

But what you need to realize is that the best thing about entrepreneurship is that you can create your business any way you want.

And if you get a mentor to help you make decisions it's basically like having a boss oversee your work – you start to lose that freedom that you really wanted.

If you constantly have people guiding you on your journey, your wins aren't really your wins and your losses aren't really your losses.

If you don't take ownership of your wins and losses, you never really get that 'OMG! I DID IT!' feeling.

And you also never learn from your mistakes because they weren't your mistakes in the first place.

You're going to make bad decisions but you'll make some great ones too.

You don't need a mentor to teach you how to be successful, especially if your goal is to live life on your own terms.

#6. Start Building Your Expertise

You don't have to be the best on day one.

But you can start building up to it.

If you consistently take the time every day to invest in your growth, you'll be amazed by your growth a year from now.

If you're running online stores, take the time to learn and test out different marketing hacks.

By sticking it out for a year, you'll likely see that you've been building up your sales.

If you're a writer, write every day for a year.

By trying out different writing styles and pumping out consistent content, you'll likely realize that you've started to amass a loyal following.

Building your expertise requires effort.

And your expertise will help you find your answer to the question of how to be successful.

#7. Stop Blocking Yourself

Roadblocks, bad days, failures, procrastination: what do they have in common?

They're all in your head.

I'm so used to roadblocks that my instant reaction is always to find the workaround.

I've done some weird stuff just to jump over obstacles.

Yesterday I had a bad day and then halfway through the day, I realized I just had a bad sleep the night before and I just started laughing. Why? Because I realized that the solution to my problem was easy. All I needed to do is go to bed earlier that night. Next day? It was like the bad day never happened.

Your success can never be blocked by an external force.

There's always a workaround solution.

And that solution almost always comes from removing a mental barrier in your head.

If you need to change anything about yourself, change your perspective.

#8. Start Doing

You can't achieve success if you haven't done anything.

There's no big financial reward just for showing up.

You need to put in the time and energy into building something.

After all, the most successful people are all creators.

Mark Zuckerberg created Facebook. Jeff Bezos created Amazon. Sara Blakely created Spanx.

And if you devote your life to being a creator, you could eventually start to see what it takes to be successful.

But it does take time and consistent effort.

I know it's easier to just put on Netflix and turn off your brain after a work day, but the results you want to see come from keeping your brain turned on after hours. By outworking those around you.

Conclusion

Being successful comes down to you.

I could list a million more tricks about how to be successful in life but if you're not willing to do the work, it won't pay off.

You've finished reading this article and so now you have two options.

Option A: You start building something: a store, a blog, an app, (fill in the blanks).

Option B: You admit to yourself that you don't really want to succeed, you only like the idea of it. And you go marathon a show on Netflix for the rest of the day.

I hope for your sake you go with Option A. I mean you've just read an article about how to be successful, I'm pretty sure you were serious about achieving success before reading it.

But if you choose Option B, I hope that you take the time to find fulfillment and happiness in whatever you do. And I hope years from now, you're smiling knowing that you have no regrets.

What Are The 5 Keys To Success?

#1. Stop Looking for the Silver Bullet

#2. Start Creating Better Goals

#3. Start Building Your Expertise

#4. Stop Blocking Yourself

#5. Start Doing

Scale from 1-10, how serious are you about achieving success in your life? Let us know in the comments!

CHAPTER FIFTEEN

VISUALIZE, VISUALIZE, VISUALIZE!

Visualization = Imagining – and Achieving – Your Goals

Have you ever wondered what Olympic athletes think about right before they compete? Imagine this for a moment: they're in front of thousands, or even millions, of people. They're feeling nervous, watching their competition, and considering all the things that might go wrong and how to avoid them.

Sounds reasonable, right? After all, that's probably what we would do in their position. But well-trained athletes know that they should never visualize mistakes, especially right before a competition. Why? Because picturing, or visualizing, mistakes – imagining poor performance – increases the likelihood that the athletes will actually do those things during the event, even when they don't mean to.

Instead, most top athletes are trained to visualize their goals right before a competition. They see themselves winning the game, running the fastest race, or scoring the winning point. They're trained to "picture" what they want to happen, instead of what they don't want to happen. When they do this, their chances for success increase dramatically.

This is the power of visualization – and you, too, can use this technique every day to help you achieve your goals and dreams. In this article, we outline what visualization is, and how you can start using it in your life.

What Is Visualization?

Visualization is a simple technique that you can use to create a strong mental image of a future event. With good use of visualization, you can practice in advance for the event, so that you can prepare properly for it. And by visualizing success, you can build the self-confidence you need to perform well.

For instance, imagine you have a major job interview next week. You're nervous already, and it's easy to worry about giving poor answers to the interviewer's questions, speaking awkwardly about your past accomplishments, and forgetting your letters of recommendation.

Does this sound familiar? We've all probably experienced negative thinking like this.

However, instead of thinking negatively, you could use visualization to imagine that the interview goes well. You could picture yourself talking confidently, easily describing all of your past achievements, and providing letters of recommendation to the interviewer. That vision feels a lot better, doesn't it?

Visualization offers several benefits:

Visualizing outcomes that you want can increase your confidence. "Seeing" yourself succeed helps you believe that it can – and will – happen.

Visualization helps you "practice" success. When you imagine every step of an event or activity going well, you get your mind and body ready to take those steps in real life.

Anyone can benefit from visualization. You don't have to be a life coach or personal development expert to use visualization to achieve your goals.

How to Use Visualization to Achieve Your Goals

The great thing about visualization is that you can use it in so many areas of your life. Do you want a promotion? Do you want to make more friends at the office? Do you want to start your own business?

Visualization can help you in all of these areas. This is why so many highly effective people use the technique to help them achieve their goals and dreams.

Follow these steps to start visualizing your goals.

1. Decide What You Want

What do you want to focus on? Pick one dream or goal to start visualizing. For example, visualize a successful outcome of the presentation you're going to give next week.

2. Picture the Scene

Start imagining the exact scene. Don't be vague or unclear – the more specific you are, and the more details you imagine, the better the visualization will work for you.

Picture the scene as if you were there. What color are the walls? What are you wearing? Who is in the room with you?

Make sure you use all of your senses in the visualization exercise. Sight, sound, taste, smell, touch – include them all so that you really bring your vision to life.

In our example, imagine yourself standing in front of the group. Picture each team member's face, and what each person is wearing. Hear the sound of papers being moved around, the smell of fresh coffee, the sight of sunshine coming in through the office windows.

Also, imagine what you're feeling and experiencing. You're confident and excited about the presentation you're about to give. You know that your team members will enjoy what you have to say, and will find value in the information you share with them. You're really looking forward to getting started.

3. Imagine Each Step Toward Your Successful Conclusion

What will you have to do to make sure your presentation is successful?

Identify each step that must take place for you to achieve your goal. And start picturing each step as part of your visualization exercise.

For example, your presentation will open with an introduction. So, visualize yourself explaining to the group why you're giving the presentation, and what they'll get out of it.

Visualize the talking points you'll use, and what you'll say for each slide. Picture your hand motions, and imagine looking directly at everyone as you speak.

Go through the entire presentation in your mind, focusing on each step and how you'll feel. Remember, always focus on what you want, not on what you don't want. You want to feel relaxed and confident, not nervous or forgetful. So, focus on the positive feelings, and avoid the negative ones.

4. Visualize Daily

If your presentation is two weeks away, aim to do a complete visualization at least once a day until the actual day arrives.

It's important to be consistent, because regular visualization can convince your brain that what you imagine is actually the truth. The more you visualize something, the stronger that vision becomes – and the higher the likelihood that you'll get what you want. Why? Because you've done it already.

Visualizing daily is just like training for a marathon, or perfecting a golf swing. The more you practice, the more familiar your body (or your mind) will become with those specific "motions." You're literally training your mind for a successful outcome.

The great thing about visualization is that you can do it anywhere: on the train to and from work, at night before you go to bed, or while you're having your morning coffee.

More Visualization Tips

Here are more things to try with visualization:

Choose a quiet environment. Do your visualization exercises in a quiet place. This allows you to focus on the experience and get the greatest benefit from it. Every time you're interrupted, it takes longer to get back into the full visualization.

Write down one sentence that describes the outcome you want. Post this statement somewhere that's easily visible, on or near your desk. This keeps the positive outcome right in front of you, where you'll think about it often. If you can, repeat the sentence out loud several times a day.

Find an image that represents your visualization. In our presentation example, it might be a picture of someone talking confidently in front of a group. Put this image someplace that's easily visible – on your desk, saved on your computer's wallpaper, and so on. This is another tool to help you visualize your desired outcome while you're working.

Key Points

Visualization is a useful technique that helps you reach your goals and live your dreams. It works by getting your mind and body ready for what you want to happen – and, just like exercise, the more you do it, the stronger it becomes.

Aim to practice your visualization exercises daily in a quiet place, and make sure your visualizations are as detailed as possible. Remember – always focus on what you want to happen, not on what you don't want to happen.